Cultures of the World! Australia, New Zealand & Papua New Guinea Culture for Kids
Children's Cultural Studies Books

PROFESSOR GUSTO
EDUCATIONAL & INFORMATIVE BOOKS FOR CHILDREN
(PRE-K / K-12)

What do you know of Australia, New Zealand and Papua New Guinea? These countries belong to the Australian subcontinent and Oceania.

Culture of Australia- What is an Aussie?

Australians are admired for their down-to-earth personalities. Australians value sincerity and authenticity. They prefer to be with people who are humble, modest, and with a sense of humor. They don't boast of their academic and other achievements.

Australian greetings are casual and relaxed. A handshake and smile will do. They usually call you by your first name.

On birthdays and Christmas, family members often exchange small gifts. Trades people are most likely given gifts as well. Australians open their gifts when they receive them.

Many invitations are for barbeques. Arrive on time when invited to a dinner. Contact the hostess ahead of time and ask if she would like you to bring something for the meal.

They are punctual in business meetings. Meetings are done in relaxed manner. Don't exaggerate when making business presentations.

Culture of
New Zealand-
Meet the
Kiwis and
Maoris!

People in New Zealand are outgoing and friendly. They are known to be hospitable, too. They are easy to get to know. They greet and offer assistance to strangers. They call one another by their first names.

New Zealanders dress casually, but neatly. Most of their restaurants don't have dress codes. However, business dress is conservative.

New Zealand has no formal social structure. Wealth and social status are not important to them. They are proud of their achievements and believe that there are opportunities for everyone.

If a meeting is with a tribal group, welcoming protocols have to be observed. The protocols, called powhiri, should be practiced before the event. It is a formal welcome that takes place on a Marae, or meeting grounds.

Bring a small gift such as chocolates and flowers once invited. The gifts should not be lavish. They open their gifts upon receiving them.

Culture of Papua New Guinea- Meet the Papuans!

Papua New Guinea has diverse populations. It has more than 700 languages spoken.

It is a land of traditional people living in subsistence style. Most of its inhabitants are dependent on subsistence farming. Women are responsible for gardening and caring for young children.

The colorful Huli tribe living the southern highlands of Hela Province is part of the country's diverse cultures. This tribe use colorful clay as their traditional body decoration. On the other hand, the people of the Sepik region have painful skin cutting to create patterns of scars on their backs. This symbolizes strength and power.

The proud people of Papua New Guinea showcase their traditional customs and beliefs by having cultural shows and festivals. They do dancing and singing.

There is much
more to know
about the culture
of Australia,
New Zealand
and Papua
New Guinea.
Research and
have fun!

Made in the USA
San Bernardino, CA
24 October 2016